A Sampler of
Curriculum Standards for Social Studies

Expectations of Excellence

National Council for the Social Studies

Excerpted from the original by
Walter C. Parker and John Jarolimek

Allyn & Bacon
is an imprint of

Boston • New York • San Francisco
Mexico City • Montreal • Toronto • London • Madrid • Munich • Paris
Hong Kong • Singapore • Tokyo • Cape Town • Sydney

KH

ISBN-10: 0-13-501852-8
ISBN-13: 978-0-13-501852-1

Printed in the United States of America

10 9 8 7 6 5 4 3 2   **RRD-VA** 12 11 10 09 08

Allyn & Bacon
is an imprint of

10/07/10

INTRODUCTION TO THE SAMPLER

We present here excerpts from *Expectations of Excellence: Curriculum Standards for Social Studies*. These standards were developed by a task force of the National Council for the Social Studies in 1994 to answer the question. What should students know in the realm of social studies and when should they know it? They incorporate learning experiences from many disciplines—history, geography, anthropology, the humanities, and so forth. Accordingly, "teachers and curriculum designers are encouraged first to establish their program frameworks using the social studies standards as a guide, and then to use the standards from history, geography, civics, economics, and others to guide the development of grade level strands and courses."[1]

The *Curriculum Standards for Social Studies* book has three components. First, there are ten thematic statements, from "culture" to "civic ideals." Second, there are performance expectations for three levels: the early grades, middle grades, and high school. These describe more specifically the targets, that is, the "knowledge, skills, scholarly perspectives, and commitments to American democratic ideals" that students should be able to display at the three developmental levels. (Such levels are often called *benchmarks*.) Third, there are classroom activities, also called vignettes, related to each theme. Two or three vignettes are given for each theme at each of the three grade levels.

The book, *Curriculum Standards for Social Studies*, contains 178 pages from which we have excerpted the material in this *Sampler*. We encourage readers to examine the complete version. It can probably be found in the university's curriculum library, and an order form is located in this *Sampler*. We also encourage readers to become members of the National Council for the Social Studies, the primary professional organization and network for teachers who are especially interested in the social studies. NCSS members not only receive a discount on the *Curriculum Standards for Social Studies* book, but numerous benefits and resources, not the least of which are opportunities for foreign travel with other teachers, local and national teachers' workshops, news about curriculum resources, and a subscription to the quarterly journal of social studies teaching ideas, *Social Studies and the Young Learner*.

The contents of this *Sampler* are:

We hope you find the contents stimulating, and that you will, at some point, examine a copy of the complete version.

Walter C. Parker
John Jarolimek
Seattle, Washington

---

[1] *Expectations of Excellence: Curriculum Standards for Social Studies,* p. vii.

www.socialstudies.org
National Council for the
Social Studies

Are **you** *a member?*

NCSS offers you the opportunity to learn and grow in your career by offering the following member benefits:

- Publications
- State and Local Councils
- Annual Conference
- Information Services
- Legislative Network
- Leadership
- Insurance and Credit Card
- Internet Resources

With members in all fifty states and more than sixty-nine countries, NCSS

- promotes the highest quality social studies curriculum and instruction at all levels
- defines and promotes the highest level of professional standards, rights, and status for educators
- communicates the rationale, substance, and value of social studies education and the condition for its effective teaching and learning

Vision, Influence, and **Professionalism**. Join NCSS and become part of an organization that

- provides a **Vision** for the future of social studies
- **Influences** the global community by preparing thoughtful citizens
- commits to **Professionalism** and sets the standards for the field

THE SOCIAL STUDIES STANDARDS

Providing leadership in the profession, NCSS has published *Expectations of Excellence: Curriculum Standards for Social Studies*, a framework for powerful social studies instruction. Excerpts are included in this *Sampler* accompanying *Social Studies in Elementary Education*, 13th ed., by Walter Parker (© 2009 by Pearson Education, Inc.)

The Standards present a model based on 10 thematic strands for achieving excellence at three distinct levels: early grades, middle grades, and high school. In addition to defining social studies and its mission, "to promote civic competence," this resource explains the purpose, organization, and utility of the 10 themes and their relationship to other standards in the field. Classroom activities and guidelines for assessing student performance are included. Appendices include the Essential Skills for Social Studies and a statement on democratic beliefs and values.

NCSS Membership Application

▶ Your name and address

Name _____

Institution _____

Address _____

City, State, Country, ZIP or Post Code _____

Work Phone _____

Home Phone _____

Fax _____

E-Mail _____

▶ Your sponsor

If a colleague encouraged you to join NCSS, please provide his/her name and member number:

▶ Choose a membership level

☐ New membership ☐ Renewal Member number: _____

Comprehensive: Includes your choice of *Social Education* or *Social Studies and the Young Learner*, plus *Middle Level Learning*, *TSSP*, and bulletins; Conference discounts and all other membership benefits.

Choose one: ☐ Individual $70 ☐ Institution $95

Regular: Includes your choice of *Social Education* or *Social Studies and the Young Learner*, plus *Middle Level Learning* and *TSSP*; Conference discounts and other membership benefits.

Choose one: ☐ Individual $59 ☐ Institution $79

International: International membership includes membership in the International Assembly associated group. Additional mailing charges apply, see below. Available only to individuals living outside the U.S.

Choose one: ☐ Regular $59 ☐ Comprehensive $70

First Year Teacher: Available to classroom teachers in their first year of paid employment as a teacher. Includes benefits of regular membership.

Choose one: ☐ Individual $33

Student or Retired: Includes your choice of *Social Education* or *Social Studies and the Young Learner*, plus *Middle Level Learning* and *TSSP*; Conference discounts and other membership benefits. Available to retired persons and full-time students. Students must provide the name of the institution and the signature of the instructor.

Choose one: ☐ Retired $33 ☐ Student $33

Name of institution _____

Instructor signature _____

Expected graduation date _____

▶ Join an NCSS Associated Group

These memberships run concurrently with NCSS membership, which is REQUIRED. They are NOT available to institutions.

College and University Faculty Assembly (CUFA)	☐ Reg. $45	☐ Student $15
Council of State Social Studies Specialists (CS4)	☐ Regular $30	
National Social Studies Supervisors Association (NSSSA)		☐ Regular $35
International Assembly	☐ Regular $15	
Social Science Education Consortium (SSEC)	☐ Regular $40	

▶ Choose a journal Choose one journal you wish to receive as a member benefit:

☐ 7 issues of *Social Education*
☐ 4 issues of *Social Studies and the Young Learner* plus
     2 issues (September and May/June) of *Social Education*

▶ Mailing List ☐ From time to time, NCSS makes available our membership list to carefully selected companies or organizations serving social studies educators. If you wish to be excluded from such lists, please check this box.

▶ Additional subscriptions

☐ 7 issues of *Social Education* (INSTITUTIONS ONLY): $64
☐ 4 issues of *Social Studies and the Young Learner* (MEMBERS ONLY): $20
☐ 4 issues of *Social Studies and the Young Learner* (INSTITUTIONS ONLY): $39
☐ 4 issues of *Theory and Research in Social Education* (INSTITUTIONS & NON-MEMBERS): $79

▶ About You

So that we can better tailor our programs to the needs of our members, please provide the following information:

Level:
☐ Elementary
☐ Middle School
☐ Junior High
☐ High School
☐ K–12
☐ College/University
☐ Business

Age:
☐ 25–36
☐ 37–46
☐ 47–56
☐ 57–65
☐ Older than 65

Interest:
☐ U.S. History
☐ World History
☐ Sociology/Psych.
☐ Geography
☐ Anthropology
☐ Political Science
☐ Social Studies
☐ Economics
☐ Global Studies
☐ Government/ Civics

NCSS seeks information about minority members in order to increase their participation in the organization.

Ethnicity:
☐ Asian/Pacific Islander
☐ Black/African Amer.
☐ Latino/Hispanic
☐ Native American
☐ White/European
Other *(Please specify):*

▶ Payment information

NCSS Membership:	$
Associated Group Membership:	$
Foreign Postage (EXCEPT CANADA & MEXICO) add $10:	$
Contribution to NCSS Legal Defense Fund:	$
Contribution to FASSE Fund:	$
Earmark my FASSE contribution for:	

☐ Christa McAullife Award   ☐ General Fund

Total Due (U.S. DOLLARS):	$

Choose one: ☐ American Express   ☐ MasterCard   ☐ VISA
                    ☐ Check payable to NCSS   ☐ Educational Purchase Order

Card Number: _____

Expiration Date _____ Phone: _____

Signature _____

NCSS

Please return this application with payment to:
NCSS Membership, P.O. Box 79078, Baltimore, MD 21279-0078
Phone 301 588-1800   Toll free 1 800 296-7840
Fax 301 588-2049   www.ncss.org/membership

Expectations of Excellence

CURRICULUM STANDARDS FOR SOCIAL STUDIES

Developed by
National Council for the Social Studies
Washington, D.C., 1994

Task Force:

Donald Schneider, Chair
Susan A. Adler
R. Beery
Gloria Ladson-Billings
William R. Fernekes
Michael Haroonian
Mary A. McFarland
Gerald Marker
Marjorie A. Montgomery
Pat Nickell
Corrinne Tevis

I. PURPOSE AND ORGANIZATION

What Is the Purpose of the Social Studies Standards?

Our world is changing rapidly. Students in our schools today, who will be the citizens of the twenty-first century, are living and learning in the midst of a knowledge explosion unlike any humankind has ever experienced. Because schools and teachers cannot teach everything and because students cannot learn all there is to know, this document focuses on three purposes for these standards. The social studies standards should:

1. serve as a framework for K–12 social studies program design through the use of ten thematic strands;
2. serve as a guide for curriculum decisions by providing performance expectations regarding knowledge, processes, and attitudes essential for all students; and
3. provide examples of classroom practice to guide teachers in designing instruction to help students meet performance expectations.

These social studies standards provide criteria for making decisions as curriculum planners and teachers address such issues as why teach social studies, what to include in the curriculum, how to teach it well to all students, and how to assess whether or not students are able to apply what they have learned. The ten thematic curriculum standards and accompanying sets of student performance expectations constitute an irreducible minimum of what is essential in social studies. Along with the examples of classroom practice, these standards and performance expectations help answer the following questions:

- How can the social studies curriculum help students construct an accurate and positive view of citizenship and become citizens able to address persistent issues, promote civic ideals and practices, and improve our democratic republic?

- What content themes are essential to the curriculum at every level (early, middle, and high school) because they address societal expectations and the needs of young future citizens and are drawn from disciplines and fields related to social studies and from other disciplines and fields that are natural allies of social studies?

- What are the student performance expectations at early, middle, and high school levels for knowledge, skills, attitudes, civic ideals, and practices that encompass social studies as an integrative field?

- How can learning opportunities be structured at each school level to help students meet social studies performance expectations?

- How might performance expectations be assessed to show that students have constructed an understanding that allows them to demonstrate and apply what they have learned?

How Are the Social Studies Standards Organized?

The social studies standards present, in the next chapters of this document, a set of ten thematically based curriculum standards, corresponding sets of performance expectations, and illustrations of exemplary teaching and learning to foster student achievement of the standards at each school level.

A **curriculum standard** is a statement of what should occur programmatically in the formal schooling process; it provides a guiding vision of content and purpose. The social studies curriculum standards, designated by roman numerals, are expressed in thematic statements that begin: "Social studies programs should include experiences that provide for the study of . . . ." These curriculum experiences should enable students to exhibit the knowledge, skills, scholarly perspectives, and commitments to American democratic ideals identified in the **performance expectations.**

For each school level, two or three (in this *Sampler*, one) examples of **classroom activities** related to each theme appear in the "Standards into Practice" chapters. In each case, the performance expectations addressed by the example are identified.

Since these themes are interdisciplinary, there is often a close relationship among performance expectations across the curriculum standards. To show these connections, roman numerals representing related themes are cross-referenced in the "Standards into Practice" chapters.

The ten themes that serve as organizing strands for the social studies curriculum at every school level are:

I	Culture
II	Time, Continuity, and Change
III	People, Places, and Environments
IV	Individual Development and Identity
V	Individuals, Groups, and Institutions
VI	Power, Authority, and Governance
VII	Production, Distribution, and Consumption
VIII	Science, Technology, and Society
IX	Global Connections
X	Civic Ideals and Practices

Two features of these curriculum strands are especially important. First, they are interrelated. To understand culture, for example, students need to understand time, continuity, and change; the relationship among people, places, and environments; and civic ideals and practices. To understand power, authority, and governance, students need to understand the relationship among culture; people, places, and environments; and individuals, groups, and institutions.

Second, the thematic strands draw from all of the social science disciplines and other related disciplines and fields of scholarly study to build a framework for social studies curriculum design. The ten themes thus present a holistic framework for state and local curriculum standards. To further enhance the curriculum design, social studies educators are encouraged to seek detailed content from standards developed for history, geography, civics, economics, and other fields.

II. TEN THEMATIC STRANDS IN SOCIAL STUDIES

I   **Culture.** The study of culture prepares students to answer questions such as: What are the common characteristics of different cultures? How do belief systems, such as religion or political ideals, influence other parts of the culture? How does the culture change to accommodate different ideas and beliefs? What does language tell us about the culture? In schools, this theme typically appears in units and courses dealing with geography, history, sociology, and anthropology, as well as multicultural topics across the curriculum.

II   **Time, Continuity, and Change.** Human beings seek to understand their historical roots and to locate themselves in time. Knowing how to read and reconstruct the past allows one to develop a historical perspective and to answer questions such as: Who am I? What happened in the past? How am I connected to those in the past? How has the world changed and how might it change in the future? Why does our personal sense of relatedness to the past change? This theme typically appears in courses in history and others that draw upon historical knowledge and habits.

III   **People, Places, and Environments.** The study of people, places, and human-environment interactions assists students as they create their spatial views and geographic perspectives of the world beyond their personal locations. Students need the knowledge, skills, and understanding to answer questions such as: Where are things located? Why are they located where they are? What do we mean by "region"? How do landforms change? What implications do these changes have for people? In schools, this theme typically appears in units and courses dealing with area studies and geography.

IV   **Individual Development and Identity.** Personal identity is shaped by one's culture, by groups, and by institutional influences. Students should consider such questions as: How do people learn? Why do people behave as they do? What influences how people learn, perceive, and grow? How do people meet their basic needs in a variety of contexts? How do individuals develop from youth to adulthood? In schools, this theme typically appears in units and courses dealing with psychology and anthropology.

V   **Individuals, Groups, and Institutions.** Institutions such as schools, churches, families, government agencies, and the courts play an integral role in people's lives. It is important that students learn how institutions are formed, what controls and influences them, how they influence individuals and culture, and how they are maintained or changed. Students may address questions such as: What is the role of institutions in this and other societies? How am I influenced by institutions? How do institutions change? What is my role in institutional change? In schools this theme typically appears in units and courses dealing with sociology, anthropology, psychology, political science, and history.

VI   **Power, Authority, and Governance.** Understanding the historical development of structures of power, authority, and governance and their evolving functions in contemporary U.S. society and other parts of the world is essential for developing civic competence. In exploring this theme, students confront questions such as: What is power? What forms does it take? Who holds it? How is it gained, used, and justified? What is legitimate authority? How are governments created, structured, maintained, and changed? How can individual rights be protected within the context of majority rule? In schools, this theme typically appears in units and courses dealing with government, politics, political science, history, law, and other social sciences.

VII **Production, Distribution, and Consumption.** Because people have wants that often exceed the resources available to them, a variety of ways have evolved to answer such questions as: What is to be produced? How is production to be organized? How are goods and services to be distributed? What is the most effective allocation of the factors of production (land, labor, capital, and management)? In schools, this theme typically appears in units and courses dealing with economic concepts and issues.

VIII **Science, Technology, and Society.** Modern life as we know it would be impossible without technology and the science that supports it. But technology brings with it many questions: Is new technology always better than old? What can we learn from the past about how new technologies result in broader social change, some of which is unanticipated? How can we cope with the ever-increasing pace of change? How can we manage technology so that the greatest number of people benefit from it? How can we preserve our fundamental values and beliefs in the midst of technological change? This theme draws upon the natural and physical sciences, social sciences, and the humanities, and appears in a variety of social studies courses, including history, geography, economics, civics, and government.

IX **Global Connections.** The realities of global interdependence require understanding the increasingly important and diverse global connections among world societies and the frequent tension between national interests and global priorities. Students will need to be able to address such international issues as health care, the environment, human rights, economic competition and interdependence, age-old ethnic enmities, and political and military alliances. This theme typically appears in units or courses dealing with geography, culture, and economics, but may also draw upon the natural and physical sciences and the humanities.

X **Civic Ideals and Practices.** An understanding of civic ideals and practices of citizenship is critical to full participation in society and is a central purpose of the social studies. Students confront such questions as: What is civic participation and how can I be involved? How has the meaning of citizenship evolved? What is the balance between rights and responsibilities? What is the role of the citizen in the community and the nation, and as a member of the world community? How can I make a positive difference? In schools, this theme typically appears in units or courses dealing with history, political science, cultural anthropology, and fields such as global studies, law-related education, and the humanities.

III. STANDARDS INTO PRACTICE: EXAMPLES FOR THE EARLY GRADES

Early Grades

 Culture

Social studies programs should include experiences that provide for the study of *culture and cultural diversity*, so that the learner can:

Performance Expectations	Related Themes
a. explore and describe similarities and differences in the ways groups, societies, and cultures address similar human needs and concerns;	
b. give examples of how experiences may be interpreted differently by people from diverse cultural perspectives and frames of reference;	
c. describe ways in which language, stories, folktales, music, and artistic creations serve as expressions of culture and influence behavior of people living in a particular culture;	
d. compare ways in which people from different cultures think about and deal with their physical environment and social conditions;	
e. give examples and describe the importance of cultural unity and diversity within and across groups.	

FOCUS ON THE CLASSROOM: STANDARDS INTO PRACTICE

Performance Expectations: a, b, d

Carlene Jackson is an active member of her state's Geographic Alliance and enjoys participating in its institute's and staff development activities. This year she has worked with several primary teachers in her district to revise and improve the elementary social studies program. An ongoing concern of the intermediate teachers is the failure of students in the early grades to develop geography understanding. Jackson has volunteered to pilot the new program in her first grade class.

Before the first day of school, Jackson looks over her class list, inferring from the children's surnames that she will have students of Mexican, Vietnamese, and Korean ancestry. She also knows that, because of the general population of the school, she will have students of African-American and European-American backgrounds. This rich mix of cultural backgrounds provides Jackson with many opportunities to expose her students to experiences that increase their geographic knowledge and skills and their cultural understanding.

By the end of the first month of school, Jackson and her first graders decide to study and compare how families meet their basic needs of food, clothing, and shelter in their community, with how families meet their needs in Juarez, Mexico; Hanoi, Vietnam; Lagos, Nigeria; and Frankfurt, Germany. To do this, Jackson and the students create the following chart:

How Families Meet Basic Needs

Needs	Our City	Juarez	Hanoi	Lagos	Frankfurt
food					
shelter					
clothing					

Throughout the unit, Jackson and her students read books and stories, look at photos and slides, watch videos, and talk to speakers from their designated cities. The students sharpen their skills in reading, writing, and speaking, in addition to learning new geography skills such as basic map reading. For each city, they read and discuss something about its location, climate, region, and people.

By the end of the unit, Jackson's students can discuss how people in at least five different places meet their basic needs. Through students' discussion and formal writing, Jackson assesses the quality of student learning by determining if they are now more knowledgeable about how cultures meet similar needs, the ways in which societal needs are influenced by geographic characteristics, and the role of economic forces in determining how wants and needs are met.

II   *Time, Continuity, & Change*

Social studies programs should include experiences that provide for the study of *the ways human beings view themselves in and over time*, so that the learner can:

Performance Expectations   **Related Themes**

a.   demonstrate an understanding that different people may describe the same event or situation in diverse ways, citing reasons for the differences in views;

b.   demonstrate an ability to use correctly vocabulary associated with time such as past, present, future, and long ago; read and construct simple timelines; identify examples of change; and recognize examples of cause and effect relationships;

c.   compare and contrast different stories or accounts about past events, people, places, or situations, identifying how they contribute to our understanding of the past;

d.   identify and use various sources for reconstructing the past, such as documents, letters, diaries, maps, textbooks, photos, and others;

e.   demonstrate an understanding that people in different times and places view the world differently;

f.   use knowledge of facts and concepts drawn from history, along with elements of historical inquiry, to inform decision-making about, and action-taking on public issues.

FOCUS ON THE CLASSROOM: STANDARDS INTO PRACTICE

Performance Expectations: b, c, d

Luis Santos' fourth grade students are studying the Northeast region of the United States. As part of this study, the students are identifying people involved in major events associated with the Revolutionary War. Santos divides the class into six groups. He assigns each group of students a specific person (e.g., George III, Sam Frances, Elizabeth Freeman, Patrick Henry, Mercy Otis Warren, and George Washington) and asks them to develop scenes that highlight their character's contributions before, during, or after the Revolutionary War. He asks the students to establish the setting and a situation in which their character is taking the lead. Students use a variety of resource materials to assist in developing the setting and dialogue for their character and others involved in their scene.

After students develop their scenes, Santos asks them to determine the correct chronological order of the scenes and then to perform their scenes for their classmates. When all scenes have been performed, the class decides whether any additional narrator text is necessary to explain how the scenes are linked, in order to present the clearest and most accurate view of how the presentation content relates to the major events of the Revolutionary War period.

To evaluate the quality of the student performances, Santos and the students discuss these questions: Were the scenes portrayed in correct chronological order? Did each scene illustrate something important to the story? Did the scenes fit together so they told the story well? Was anything important left out? Were causes and effects clearly and accurately shown?

People, Places, & Environments

Social studies programs should include experiences that provide for the study of *people, places, and environments*, so that the learner can:

Performance Expectations   **Related Themes**

a. construct and use mental maps of locales, regions, and the world that   **IX**
demonstrate understanding of relative location, direction, size, and shape;

b. interpret, use, and distinguish various representations of the earth, such   **I**
as maps, globes, and photographs;

c. use appropriate resources, data sources, and geographic tools such as
atlases, data bases, grid systems, charts, graphs, and maps to generate,
manipulate, and interpret information;

d. estimate distance and calculate scale;

e. locate and distinguish among varying landforms and geographic features,   **IX**
such as mountains, plateaus, islands, and oceans;

f. describe and speculate about physical system changes, such as seasons,   **VIII** **IX**
climate and weather, and the water cycle;

g. describe how people create places that reflect ideas, personality, culture,   **I** **IV** **V**
and wants and needs as they design homes, playgrounds, classrooms, and
the like;

h. examine the interaction of human beings and their physical environment,   **VI** **VIII**
the use of land, building of cities, and ecosystem changes in selected locales
and regions;

i. explore ways that the earth's physical features have changed over time in   **II** **IX**
the local region and beyond and how these changes may be connected to one
another;

j. observe and speculate about social and economic effects of environmental   **I** **V** **VII**
changes and crises resulting from phenomena such as floods, storms, and
drought;

k. consider existing uses and propose and evaluate alternative uses of   **V** **VII** **VIII** **IX** **X**
resources and land in home, school, community, the region, and beyond.

FOCUS ON THE CLASSROOM: STANDARDS INTO PRACTICE

Performance Expectations: a, b, c, d

As part of learning about their community, Ginny Adams' six- and seven-year-old students are working on developing mental maps of their city, including locations of major features and services. The Bureau of Tourism has provided colorful pictorial maps which students use to "explore" the city area by area. In addition, two parents of class members have created a large plastic floor outline map which contains only information necessary for orientation.

Each day, the children work with Adams in using the city maps. They discuss new areas of the city, reading the map to determine what features and services are found there. Children who have been to the area describe what they've seen.

After getting this overview of their city, the children cluster in small groups, and each group selects a different area for a study project. Working in groups, they create pop-up maps of their area and locate them accurately on the floor map. One group creates its pop-up of the zoo area. Another creates its pop-up of the community park, which includes the new pool complex. Yet another group creates representations of the downtown library and monuments.

To evaluate the accuracy of students' mental maps of the city, each student independently draws an outline map of the metropolitan area. On this outline, they draw major streets and landmarks and mark where their special pop-up area is located. Adams assesses the students' work for accuracy of the location of the pop-ups and the quality of presentation.

IV *Individual Development & Identity*

Social studies programs should include experiences that provide for the study of *individual development and identity*, so that the learner can:

Performance Expectations

Related Themes

a. describe personal changes over time, such as those related to physical development and personal interests;

II

b. describe personal connections to place—especially place as associated with immediate surroundings;

III

c. describe the unique features of one's nuclear and extended families;

I

d. show how learning and physical development affect behavior;

e. identify and describe ways family, groups, and community influence the individual's daily life and personal choices;

I **V**

f. explore factors that contribute to one's personal identity such as interests, capabilities, and perceptions;

g. analyze a particular event to identify reasons individuals might respond to it in different ways;

I **V**

h. work independently and cooperatively to accomplish goals.

X

FOCUS ON THE CLASSROOM: STANDARDS INTO PRACTICE

Performance Expectations: e, g, h

Jan Gonzales has been reading stories to her third grade class. The stories include characters who see the same situation differently for a variety of reasons. The children have noticed and discussed the fact that the characters form their ideas about the situation based on their own experiences, beliefs, and attitudes. The class has also been studying the way U.S. courts work and has discussed how different witnesses sometimes see the same situation differently.

Now Gonzales gives the students a copy of a news photo that has several unfamiliar characters and is open to interpretation as to exactly what is happening. After each student has had a reasonable amount of time to examine the photo, it is removed from view and each child writes a description entitled "What I Saw." Gonzales emphasizes writing statements that the children are prepared to defend (as a witness would "under oath"); these would be statements of what the children believe actually happened in the news photo they observed.

Once each child has completed his or her written interpretation, students move into groups of five or six and share their written descriptions. They take note of the differences they hear from one "witness's" version to another's.

The children then prepare individual written statements, describing two or three discrepancies noted among the accounts offered in their group and explaining why they believe the discrepancies may have occurred. Criteria for evaluation include the child's ability to recognize and describe differences, suggest causes, and recognize that the way an individual views an incident reflects personal beliefs, experiences, and attitudes.

Gonzales plans a follow-up discussion to encourage the children to learn from each other's written responses and to ensure that the children understand how this lesson relates to the differing assumptions illustrated by the story she read to the class earlier.

Individuals, Groups, & Institutions

Social studies programs should include experiences that provide for the study of *interactions among individuals, groups, and institutions*, so that the learner can:

Performance Expectations	**Related Themes**
a. identify roles as learned behavior patterns in group situations such as student, family member, peer play group member, or club member;	Ⅰ Ⅳ
b. give examples of and explain group and institutional influences such as religious beliefs, laws, and peer pressure, on people, events, and elements of culture;	Ⅰ Ⅱ Ⅳ Ⅵ Ⅹ
c. identify examples of institutions and describe the interactions of people with institutions;	Ⅰ Ⅵ Ⅹ
d. identify and describe examples of tensions between and among individuals, groups, or institutions, and how belonging to more than one group can cause internal conflicts;	Ⅰ Ⅱ Ⅳ Ⅹ
e. identify and describe examples of tension between an individual's beliefs and government policies and laws;	Ⅱ Ⅳ Ⅵ Ⅹ
f. give examples of the role of institutions in furthering both continuity and change;	Ⅴ Ⅵ Ⅷ Ⅹ
g. show how groups and institutions work to meet individual needs and promote the common good, and identify examples of where they fail to do so.	Ⅰ Ⅱ Ⅵ Ⅹ

FOCUS ON THE CLASSROOM: STANDARDS INTO PRACTICE

Performance Expectations: b, d, e, g

Singer Marian Anderson's voice could be heard coming from Donna Ognebene's fourth grade classroom. Once the students are in their seats, Ognebene tells them about Marian Anderson's early life. She has the students listen especially for the obstacles Anderson had to overcome and how she did so. The students identify laws and customs in society that, at that time, made it difficult for an African-American woman to have her talents acknowledged. They also identify how Anderson was able to succeed and to help change some of the customs that had been obstacles for her.

In pairs, the students then research Jackie Robinson, Martin Luther King, Jr., Sacajawea, Amelia Earhart, Nelson Mandela, Tecumseh, Mother Clara Hall, and Franklin Chang-Dias. They look for obstacles each person had to overcome and how each dealt with those obstacles. Ognebene has her students prepare posters depicting the information they found about each person and then share it with the class. As students listen and question their peers, they look for common characteristics and obstacles these individuals had to face. They discover that often beliefs and customs held by certain groups can help or hurt people as they strive to use their talents. They also find that sometimes individuals can change those beliefs and customs in ways that help people in the future succeed more easily.

Ognebene evaluates the poster displays, using the criteria of accuracy, power of visual images, and clarity of organization in presenting information.

Power, Authority, & Governance

Social studies programs should include experiences that provide for the study of *how people create and change structures of power, authority, and governance*, so that the learner can:

Performance Expectations   **Related Themes**

a.   examine the rights and responsibilities of the individual in relation to   **V** **X**
his or her social group, such as family, peer group, and school class;

b.   explain the purpose of government;   **X**

c.   give examples of how government does or does not provide for needs   **I** **V** **IX**
and wants of people, establish order and security, and manage conflict;

d.   recognize how groups and organizations encourage unity and deal   **I** **V**
with diversity to maintain order and security;

e.   distinguish among local, state, and national government and identify   **X**
representative leaders at these levels such as mayor, governor, and president;

f.   identify and describe factors that contribute to cooperation and cause   **II** **V** **IX**
disputes within and among groups and nations;

g.   explore the role of technology in communications, transportation,   **VII** **VIII** **IX**
information-processing, weapons development, or other areas as it
contributes to or helps resolve conflicts;

h.   recognize and give examples of the tensions between the wants and   **II** **IX** **X**
needs of individuals and groups, and concepts such as fairness, equity,
and justice.

FOCUS ON THE CLASSROOM: STANDARDS INTO PRACTICE

Performance Expectations: a, b, c, f, h

Using the story line method, Grace Anne Heacock's third grade class has established a town they have named Countervail, in which each student has created a family, its house, and collectively a rather complex community. The bulletin board display of the town now extends along walls and tables, and students have become quite involved in the goings-on in Countervail. To the children's dismay, however, they discover one morning that there is trash in their park and graffiti scratched on fences. One family's rabbit is missing, and the new tree in front of the plaza has been cut down.

The students have come face to face with the need for laws; otherwise, nothing can be done to stop this destruction of "their" property. For the next week, students work in cooperative groups, each dealing with a different set of concerns, to begin the process of developing a legal code for the community of Countervail.

The students brainstorm with Heacock the problems created by the property destruction and suggest a list of "do's" and "don'ts" for Countervail's population. Reviewing the list, students develop ideas about what is acceptable and unacceptable behavior. They examine a set of laws in their actual town that Heacock has rewritten in simplified form, and then identify those that appear to be relevant to their case.

Heacock invites their actual town's mayor, police chief, and fire chief to visit the class. Each guest reviews the relevant laws and discusses them with the students. The students gather information from each guest and construct charts indicating responsibilities citizens in Countervail assume for each proposed law.

As a culminating activity, Heacock has students prepare a "charter of laws" for Countervail. This charter is then shared with local officials and experts on the law, who are asked to write letters or prepare videotaped responses to the student charter. The students review the adult responses and prepare journal entries about the significance of law and its importance in the community. Heacock evaluates the quality of the journal entries based upon the clarity of student language, use of examples from the case study, and inclusion of reactions to the adult responses to the student charter.

Production, Distribution, & Consumption

Social studies programs should include experiences that provide for the study of *how people organize for the production, distribution, and consumption of goods and services,* so that the learner can:

Performance Expectations	Related Themes

a. give examples that show how scarcity and choice govern our economic decisions; **I III**

b. distinguish between needs and wants; **IV**

c. identify examples of private and public goods and services; **V VI**

d. give examples of the various institutions that make up economic systems such as families, workers, banks, labor unions, government agencies; **V**

e. describe how we depend upon workers with specialized jobs and the ways in which they contribute to the production and exchange of goods and services; **V VIII**

f. describe the influence of incentives, values, traditions, and habits on economic decisions; **I II**

g. explain and demonstrate the role of money in everyday life; **I**

h. describe the relationship of price to supply and demand; **I V**

i. use economic concepts such as supply, demand, and price to help explain events in the community and nation; **I V VI**

j. apply knowledge of economic concepts in developing a response to a current local economic issue, such as how to reduce the flow of trash into a rapidly filling landfill. **V VI VIII X**

FOCUS ON THE CLASSROOM: STANDARDS INTO PRACTICE

Performance Expectations: e, i

At the beginning of a unit on economic specialization in production, Mark Moran's early primary class is divided into two teams of cookie makers. Both teams make gingerbread cookies. One team works as an assembly line, each person having a special job—rolling out the dough, cutting the basic shape, making the almond mouth, locating raisin buttons, etc. The second team works as individuals, each person creating his or her own gingerbread cookies. Both teams have the same supplies to work with.

After they have finished baking their cookies, the students examine the cookies and identify the advantages and disadvantages of each method of producing cookies. Ideas that emerge relate to division of labor, pride, creativity, independence, specialization, and quality control.

Students subsequently prepare summaries in writing about how they produced their cookies. Moran evaluates the quality of the student writing by determining how accurate the students are in detailing the production process and the extent to which evidence of key concepts is present.

In the weeks that follow this lesson, students examine other situations involving assembly line production, including a field trip to a local plant where pickup trucks are assembled.

Science, Technology, & Society

Social studies programs should include experiences that provide for the study of *relationships among science, technology, and society,* so that the learner can:

Performance Expectations   **Related Themes**

a.   identify and describe examples in which science and technology have
changed the lives of people, such as in homemaking, childcare, work,
transportation, and communication;

b.   identify and describe examples in which science and technology have
led to changes in the physical environment, such as the building of dams
and levees, offshore drilling, medicine from rain forests, and loss of rain
forests due to extraction of resources or alternative uses;

c.   describe instances in which changes in values, beliefs, and attitudes
have resulted from new scientific and technological knowledge, such as
conservation of resources and awareness of chemicals harmful to
life and the environment;

d.   identify examples of laws and policies that govern scientific
and technological applications, such as the Endangered Species
Act and environmental protection policies;

e.   suggest ways to monitor science and technology in order to protect
the physical environment, individual rights, and the common good.

FOCUS ON THE CLASSROOM: STANDARDS INTO PRACTICE

Performance Expectations: a, b, c, e

The third graders in Dodie Righi's class have established the need to study how humans change the environment. One of the issues being discussed is recycling. At lunch, one of the students, Jorge, notices that the cafeteria is serving juice in styrofoam cups. Since the students have learned that styrofoam requires the use of CFCs in the production process and that CFCs have a deleterious effect on the ozone layer, he goes to his teacher to express his concern.

Righi had been getting the class ready to take action on an environmental problem in the community, and Jorge's plea was a perfect teachable moment. While students discuss how to proceed in their cooperative learning groups, Mattie scoots to the cafeteria and copies down the address of the company that manufactures the cups. By the time Mattie returns, the groups are ready to report. Righi jots down their ideas on the overhead, and each group makes out a plan based on the ideas of the whole class. The students agree upon a plan that includes contacting the company to ask why they make cups of styrofoam and how many CFCs are released

---

in the production of each cup. They next want to find out how many styrofoam cups the school uses annually; then, they can multiply and figure out how many CFCs are released into the air as a result of the use of styrofoam cups in their cafeteria. Righi asks each student to begin keeping a folder in which he or she maintains a record of the class's work on the problem.

Righi works with the students to plan how to make phone calls to businesses to get information effectively and how to write a business letter. After obtaining information, the students graph their data to show the impact of the styrofoam cups they consumed. The students use an electronic bulletin board to gather additional information, as well as CD-ROMs in the school media center and the local library to get more information on the manufacture of styrofoam.

When they have garthered enough information, the class discusses what they should do about it. Righi suggests that they explore alternatives to using the styrofoam cups. They go through the same information-gathering process, checking out paper cups and the feasibility of using their own cups and leaving them in their cubbies. The latter means that they need to talk with the Director of Public Health to find out about health standards. She explains to them the temperature at which they need to wash their own cups and the energy needed to purify, pump, and heat that water.

After looking at all the information, the students decide that the best solution is to use paper, rather than styrofoam, cups for snacks and lunches. The head of the cafeteria says that she needs a directive from the school board to make the change. With Righi's help, Roger calls the school board secretary and secures a spot on the agenda for the next meeting. For that week, the students work very hard in selecting the information they want to give the board and the visuals they want to show. The students prepare a videotape to use in an assembly program they present to the whole school and later to the board. They explain their efforts and analyze how their work can serve as a model for other student action strategies.

Righi evaluates their presentation on the clarity with which they represented the strategies and their ability to critique strategies for effectiveness. She also asks students to hand in their folders containing their record of all class activities related to their problem. She evaluates the folders on completeness of information, spelling, and grammar. She makes special notes on how well each student captures the nature of the problem on which the class worked, i.e., how various choices people make have different effects on the environment.

After the presentation to the school board, the board votes to switch to paper cups. Buoyed by their success, the students make the same presentation to the town council in an effort to get them to use paper cups in government offices.

Global Connections

Social studies programs should include experiences that provide for the study of *global connections and interdependence* so that the learner can:

Performance Expectations   **Related Themes**

a.   explore ways that language, art, music, belief systems, and other cultural
elements may facilitate global understanding or lead to misunderstanding;

b.   give examples of conflict, cooperation, and interdependence among
individuals, groups, and nations;

c.   examine the effects of changing technologies on the global community;

d.   explore causes, consequences, and possible solutions to persistent,
contemporary, and emerging global issues, such as pollution and endangered
species;

e.   examine the relationships and tensions between personal wants and needs
and various global concerns, such as use of imported oil, land use, and
environmental protection;

f.   investigate concerns, issues, standards, and conflicts related to universal
human rights, such as the treatment of children, religious groups, and effects
of war.

FOCUS ON THE CLASSROOM: STANDARDS INTO PRACTICE

Performance Expectations: d, e, f

For their heritage unit, the children in Deanna Parker's combined first and second grade class interview their parents, grandparents, and relatives to find out what country or region their family may have emigrated from and when. They ask their relatives what they know about the family's former homeland and what it was like when the family left it for the United States. Those students who are unable to identify an original homeland are asked to join with another child who has. They create maps indicating their families' places of origin and movements over time, and gather additional information from the library and other resources about the cultural heritage of the homeland.

As the year progresses, students gather news stories about the country or region of their heritage to learn about ways it has changed. Parker gives special emphasis to similarities and differences of the regions or countries with the United States and also emphasizes problems and issues facing these countries, helping the children understand the relationship between these and problems and issues faced in the United States and how each country deals with these concerns.

As a culmination activity, students working individually or in groups build a desk-top museum to exhibit information they have gathered about the region or country of their ancestors. The librarian/media specialist and art and music teachers assist students with gathering arts resources and adding artistic touches to exhibits. Parents and other volunteers are invited to help in this project. Parents, relatives, special guests, and other students are invited to a schoolwide open house to view the exhibits.

X *Civic Ideals & Practices*

Social studies programs should include experiences that provide for the study of *the ideals, principles, and practices of citizenship in a democratic republic,* so that the learner can:

Performance Expectations	Related Themes

Performance Expectations   **Related Themes**

a.   identify key ideals of the United States' democratic republican form of government, such as individual human dignity, liberty, justice, equality, and the rule of law, and discuss their application in specific situations;   **II   V   VI**

b.   identify examples of rights and responsibilities of citizens;   **II**

c.   locate, access, organize, and apply information about an issue of public concern from multiple points of view;   **I   II   V   IX**

d.   identify and practice selected forms of civic discussion and participation consistent with the ideals of citizens in a democratic republic;   **II   V   VI**

e.   explain actions citizens can take to influence public policy decisions;   **V   VI**

f.   recognize that a variety of formal and informal actors influence and shape public policy;   **V   VI**

g.   examine the influence of public opinion on personal decision making and government policy on public issues;   **V   VI**

h.   explain how public policies and citizen behaviors may or may not reflect the stated ideals of a democratic republican form of government;   **II   V   VI**

i.   describe how public policies are used to address issues of public concern;   **VI**

j.   recognize and interpret how the "common good" can be strengthened through various forms of citizen action.   **II   V   VI**

FOCUS ON THE CLASSROOM: STANDARDS INTO PRACTICE

Performance Expectations: a, c, d, e, i, j

   Ellen Stein's fourth grade class is studying how its local community government operates to solve problems of public concern. Their school is located next to an abandoned factory, which is being considered as a site for either a shopping center or a public park. Citizens holding different perspectives have argued and debated the merits of the two proposals in the media, and many of the students' parents have strong opinions about the issue. Because of the local concerns, the students want to study the issue, gather information, think about the consequences of different positions, and make their opinions heard.

Stein invites representatives from different groups in the community who will influence the decision to talk with students. People invited are the mayor, members of the planning board, the town council, the chamber of commerce, various citizens' groups, and a number of residents who live in the surrounding neighborhood. For each visit, small groups of students in the class are designated as information gatherers, recorders of answers to questions, and questioners. After the visits, students examine the positions of the different groups, and the class develops a list of questions, issues, and concerns to be sent along with "thank you" letters to the visitors. The students also discuss what each community group's priorities appear to be and how their community may be affected by the differing priorities of the groups.

After further information gathering and review of the pros and cons of several alternatives, the class decides to prepare a poster campaign, supporting the alternatives it believes are most beneficial for the interests of the entire community. Stein helps the students consider the elements that make effective posters attention-grabbing qualities, visuals, wording that conveys a clear message, accuracy, evidence supporting the position presented, and persuasiveness. After developing their individual posters, students select the best poster using the qualities previously identified. Students invite the local newspaper to send a reporter and photographer to see the poster display in their school, take photos, and write an article. They also obtain permission to place the display in the regional library.

IV. STANDARDS INTO PRACTICE: EXAMPLES FOR THE MIDDLE GRADES

Middle Grades

 Culture

Social studies programs should include experiences that provide for the study of *culture and cultural diversity*, so that the learner can:

Performance Expectations   **Related Themes**

a. compare similarities and differences in the ways groups, societies, and cultures meet human needs and concerns;   **II III V**

b. explain how information and experiences may be interpreted by people from diverse cultural perspectives and frames of reference;   **II III IV V IX**

c. explain and give examples of how language, literature, the arts, architecture, other artifacts, traditions, beliefs, values, and behaviors contribute to the development and transmission of culture;   **II III V IX**

d. explain why individuals and groups respond differently to their physical and social environments and/or changes to them on the basis of shared assumptions, values, and beliefs;   **II III V**

e. articulate the implications of cultural diversity, as well as cohesion, within and across groups.   **II III V IX**

FOCUS ON THE CLASSROOM: STANDARDS INTO PRACTICE

Performance Expectations: a, b, c, e

Chanda Winston's eighth grade students are studying the Americans before European contact. One student, Benjamin Whitehorse, remarks that the class used the term "Indian" in such a general way that it suggested no difference among the many tribes that inhabited the continent. "You're right," says Winston. "While I'm sure you have heard of many different tribes and recognize that a variety of factors shaped their group norms, customs, and traditions, it is easy for us to forget and begin talking in generalities. Let's do something about that."

At their next class session, Winston paraphrases her discussion with Benjamin and passes out a copy of the poem "On the Pulse of Morning," written and read by Maya Angelou at the 1993 Clinton Presidential Inauguration. She draws their attention to the section that reads, "You, who gave me my first name, you Pawnee, Apache, Seneca, you Cherokee nation."

"Why do you think the poet named these Indian groups separately? Why didn't she just say Indians?" asks Winston. The students suggest a variety of reasons including the poet's attempt to recognize American Indians as distinct cultural groups and the use of listing as a literary device.

Winston then lists on the board the four groups that were mentioned in the poem and adds the Arawak, whom Columbus first encountered. She divides the class into groups to research general questions about the groups: their geographic regions, what we know about them before European contact, what we know about them after European contact, and what we know about their contemporary status with particular emphasis on architecture, technology, customs, and celebrations. Each group is to provide information for a retrieval chart that Winston outlines.

When the students complete the chart, they recognize that the various tribes have similarities and many differences. They also recognize that their own thinking about American Indians has been limited. Even their vocabulary is affected by their research.

"We now realize that there is a difference between tribes, bands, and federations," said one student. "How would you like us to be different as a result of this study?" asks Winston. "Well," suggests a student, "we can make it a rule—well, I guess I mean a practice—that whenever possible we will refer to American Indians by specific tribal names. You know, like we'll say the Nez Perce or the Algonquin, like that." Another student chimes in, "I think we need to do this for everybody. We tend to do the same with Asians. We should differentiate between Chinese, Malaysians, Japanese, Vietnamese, and others."

This is just what Winston wants to hear. She asks the students to use the same techniques to develop a chart for Asians. She particularly seeks evidence of students' ability to distinguish similarities and differences before and after European contact and the Asian groups' contemporary status with particular emphasis on architecture, technology, customs, and celebrations, elements that students identified in their initial class discussion as likely areas of cross-cultural impact.

II *Time, Continuity, & Change*

Social studies programs should include experiences that provide for the study of *the ways human beings view themselves in and over time*, so that the learner can:

Performance Expectations   **Related Themes**

a.   demonstrate an understanding that different scholars may describe the   **I** **III** **V**
same event or situation in different ways but must provide reasons or evidence
for their views;

b.   identify and use key concepts such as chronology, causality, change,   **I** **III** **V** **VIII**
conflict, and complexity to explain, analyze, and show connections among
patterns of historical change and continuity;

c.   identify and describe selected historical periods and patterns of change   **I** **V** **VIII** **X**
within and across cultures, such as the rise of civilizations, the development
of transportation systems, the growth and breakdown of colonial systems,
and others;

d.   identify and use processes important to reconstructing and reinterpreting   **I** **III** **X**
the past, such as using a variety of sources, providing, validating, and
weighing evidence for claims, checking credibility of sources, and
searching for causality;

e.   develop critical sensitivities such as empathy and skepticism regarding   **I** **III** **V** **VI** **VII**
attitudes, values, and behaviors of people in different historical contexts;   **VIII** **IX**

f.   use knowledge of facts and concepts drawn from history, along with   **V** **VI** **VII** **VIII** **IX**
methods of historical inquiry, to inform decision-making about, and   **X**
action-taking on public issues.

FOCUS ON THE CLASSROOM: STANDARDS INTO PRACTICE

Performance Expectations: a, b, c, d, e, f

   Matt Laufer's eighth grade class has been studying the American Revolution by reading various accounts of the events leading up to the outbreak of the war, including the textbook. In addition to these historical accounts, half the class has been assigned to read *Johnny Tremain* (a romanticized view of the American Revolution from the point of view of the Patriots), while the other half has read *My Brother Sam Is Dead* (which presents the perspectives of loyalists, rebels, pacifists, and undecided colonists).

After students complete the novels, Laufer assigns students to work in small groups, according to which book they read. Each group is to discuss the following questions:

(1) According to each novel, what was the American Revolution like for ordinary people in colonial America?

(2) What are the differences in the point of view of each author?

(3) Based on these two stories, what conclusions might you draw about the dilemmas colonial Americans faced at the outbreak of war? What sources could you use to confirm your hypotheses?

(4) Since one event may be portrayed in different ways, what might a citizen today do to get an accurate view of a contemporary issue?

Following their group discussions, each student hands in his or her own answers to the questions discussed by the group.

To assess their understanding of multiple perspectives, Laufer has his students work with partners or in small groups, gathering information about a contemporary issue from different perspectives. The students develop a list of criteria for assessing the information they gather, emphasizing credibility, detection of bias, accuracy of information, balance in points of view, and ways to prove the validity of claims and generalizations. Each student then prepares a news story and an editorial about the issue. After getting feedback and editorial assistance from their writing groups, each student prepares a final copy that Laufer uses for the final assessment. The criteria he uses for evaluation are: (1) the ability to list and apply at least three criteria for evaluating information, (2) providing credible evidence for claims made about events and conditions, and (3) providing reasonable and accurate support for the editorial position.

People, Places, & Environments

Social studies programs should include experiences that provide for the study of *people, places, and environments*, so that the learner can:

Performance Expectations   **Related Themes**

a.   elaborate mental maps of locales, regions, and the world that demonstrate
understanding of relative location, direction, size, and shape;

b.   create, interpret, use, and distinguish various representations of the earth,
such as maps, globes, and photographs;

c.   use appropriate resources, data sources, and geographic tools such as aerial
photographs, satellite images, geographic information systems (GIS), map
projections, and cartography to generate, manipulate, and interpret
information such as atlases, data bases, grid systems, charts, graphs,
and maps;

d.   estimate distance, calculate scale, and distinguish other geographic
relationships such as population density and spatial distribution patterns;

e.   locate and describe varying landforms and geographic features, such as
mountains, plateaus, islands, rain forests, deserts, and oceans, and explain
their relationships within the ecosystem;

f.   describe physical system changes such as seasons, climate and weather,
and the water cycle and identify geographic patterns associated with them;

g.   describe how people create places that reflect cultural values and ideals
as they build neighborhoods, parks, shopping centers, and the like;

h.   examine, interpret, and analyze physical and cultural patterns and their
interactions, such as land use, settlement patterns, cultural transmission of
customs and ideas, and ecosystem changes;

i.   describe ways that historical events have been influenced by, and have
influenced, physical and human geographic factors in local, regional,
national, and global settings;

j.   observe and speculate about social and economic effects of environmental
changes and crises resulting from phenomena such as floods, storms, and
drought;

k. propose, compare, and evaluate alternative uses of land and resources in communities, regions, nations, and the world.

FOCUS ON THE CLASSROOM: STANDARDS INTO PRACTICE

Performance Expectations: b, c, e, h

Annie Gerner has her sixth grade class use globes to expand their understanding of the idea of human migration. During this activity, she divides the class into groups representing each continent. Each group researches its continent to identify cultural minority groups that have dwelt on the continent. Gerner then has individual students from each group select one of the minority cultures identified and trace its migration patterns over time. Each group creates a large map of its continent on which students illustrate the various cultures' migration patterns in a manner that is clear and easy to understand. Each group presents its findings to the class.

Gerner assesses each group presentation on its historical and geographic accuracy and the quality of the map. Each presentation is used to determine whether students are acquiring skills and the ability to communicate and present data and ideas.

IV *Individual Development & Identity*

Social studies programs should include experiences that provide for the study of *individual development and identity*, so that the learner can:

Performance Expectations   **Related Themes**

a.   relate personal changes to social, cultural, and historical contexts;   **I** **II** **IX**

b.   describe personal connections to place—as associated with   **III**
community, nation, and world;

c.   describe the ways family, gender, ethnicity, nationality, and   **I** **V**
institutional affiliations contribute to personal identity;

d.   relate such factors as physical endowment and capabilities, learning,
motivation, personality, perception, and behavior to individual development;

e.   identify and describe ways regional, ethnic, and national   **I** **II** **III**
cultures influence individuals' daily lives;

f.   identify and describe the influence of perception, attitudes,   **I** **V**
values, and beliefs on personal identity;

g.   identify and interpret examples of stereotyping, conformity,   **I** **V**
and altruism;

h.   work independently and cooperatively to accomplish goals.   **X**

FOCUS ON THE CLASSROOM: STANDARDS INTO PRACTICE

Performance Expectations: d, f, h

   Jim Samples has been working with his seventh grade class on the importance of careful decision-making and the various factors that influence individuals' decisions. He asks students to select a recent choice of some importance to them, but one that is not too personal for public discussion and for reflection and analysis of factors they considered in reaching a decision. As examples, he suggests decisions to try out for honor band or an athletic team, not go to summer camp or to join a club. As a class, the students share the decision-making factors they came up with; these included wants and needs, talents, interests, and influence of family members, peers, or media.

   Each student, thinking of his or her own decision, charts the decision-making factors, sorting the various factors into pros and cons. Then each student assigns a weight to each influence. A weight of +3 is strongly positive; a weight of –3 is strongly negative. Each student discusses his or her choices, shows how the decision was reached, and explains what influences affected the decision and how each influence was weighted.

Clarity of the description of the choice, pro/con analysis with justifications for each weighting, the degree to which conclusions are supported by the student, and the quality of the student's presentation serve as criteria for evaluation.

V *Individuals, Groups, & Institutions*

Social studies programs should include experiences that provide for the study of *interactions among individuals, groups, and institutions*, so that the learner can:

Performance Expectations   **Related Themes**

a.   demonstrate an understanding of concepts such as role, status, and social class in describing the interactions of individuals and social groups;   **I** **IV**

b.   analyze group and institutional influences on people, events, and elements of culture;   **I** **II** **IV** **VI** **X**

c.   describe the various forms institutions take and the interactions of people with institutions;   **I** **VI** **X**

d.   identify and analyze examples of tensions between expressions of individuality and group or institutional efforts to promote social conformity;   **I** **II** **IV** **VI** **X**

e.   identify and describe examples of tensions between belief systems and government policies and laws;   **I** **II** **IV** **VI** **X**

f.   describe the role of institutions in furthering both continuity and change;   **I** **II** **VI** **VIII** **X**

g.   apply knowledge of how groups and institutions work to meet individual needs and promote the common good.   **I** **II** **VI** **X**

FOCUS ON THE CLASSROOM: STANDARDS INTO PRACTICE

Performance Expectations: c, d, f, g

Dorothy McDonald's eighth grade students are studying the pre-Civil War era. Although the students seem to be able to remember the facts of the era, they do not seem to have a sense of the interplay of individuals, groups, and institutions in bringing about societal change. McDonald decides to raise the following questions with her students: "Can individuals change society? Can groups? Can institutions?" She divides the class into three groups, one each for individuals, groups, and institutions, to investigate the question. She tells students they can answer the question any way they want, except for giving a written report. Most students are relieved to know they don't have to write a paper. However, they soon learn that they may be doing even more work to answer the question by not using the familiar format of a written report.

McDonald suggests some examples for investigation. They include Frederick Douglass, John Brown, the Grimke sisters, Harriet Beecher Stowe, representatives at the Seneca Falls Convention, state and federal courts (including the Supreme Court), Abraham Lincoln/the Presidency, and leaders of Congress. Students suggest more possibilities.

Over the next week, students research and talk with each other about how they will make their case. McDonald focuses the class on leaders of the abolitionist movement as a case study for understanding reform. At the end of the week, the three groups make presentations that support their notions about how individuals, groups, and institutions could change society. One group does a magazine exposé of the terrible conditions endured by slaves in the South. A second group does a panel presentation featuring well-known individuals from the era who explain how they thought their work would make a better society. The third group convenes a meeting of people who were working for suffrage rights for women and African-Americans.

The overwhelming conclusion of the class is that all three—individuals, groups, and institutions—can and do make changes in the society. As a follow up, McDonald asks students to develop a list in each category of present-day people who are working for social change. McDonald assesses the quality of the group projects by determining how effectively they use accurate historical information, the degree to which they evaluate the strengths and weaknesses of reform efforts, and the clarity and logical development of the arguments used to reach conclusions.

VI *Power, Authority, & Governance*

Social studies programs should include experiences that provide for the study of *how people create and change structures of power, authority, and governance*, so that the learner can:

Performance Expectations   **Related Themes**

a. examine persistent issues involving the rights, roles, and status of the   **II** **V** **X**
individual in relation to the general welfare;

b. describe the purpose of government and how its powers are acquired,   **X**
used, and justified;

c. analyze and explain ideas and governmental mechanisms to meet needs   **I** **V** **IX**
and wants of citizens, regulate territory, manage conflict, and establish order
and security;

d. describe the ways nations and organizations respond to forces of unity   **I** **II** **V**
and diversity affecting order and security;

e. identify and describe the basic features of the political system in the   **X**
United States, and identify representative leaders from various levels and
branches of government;

f. explain conditions, actions, and motivations that contribute to conflict   **II** **IX**
and cooperation within and among nations;

g. describe and analyze the role of technology in communications,   **VII** **VIII** **IX**
transportation, information-processing, weapons development, or other
areas as it contributes to, or helps resolve conflicts;

h. explain and apply concepts such as power, role, status, justice, and   **I** **II** **V**
influence to the examination of persistent issues and social problems;

i. give examples and explain how governments attempt to achieve their   **IX** **X**
stated ideals at home and abroad.

FOCUS ON THE CLASSROOM: STANDARDS INTO PRACTICE

Performance Expectations: b, c, d, f, h, i
    John Crawford's fifth grade class is nearing the end of a unit on how governments have used their power to maintain order and stability. They have already read a case study of how the British tried to control the American colonists prior to the Revolutionary War and have viewed videotapes showing how the former

Soviet Union dealt with the Baltic Republics when they attempted to break away and declare their independence. During their discussions, the students develop a chart listing different ways that governments responded in such situations and which specific governing philosophies are most consistent with the various choices.

To help students see how these various choices led to quite different results, Crawford introduces a computer simulation on revolutions. The simulation involves a hypothetical state threatening to break away from its republic. Crawford organizes the students into teams after helping them set their priorities among several choices for action. As teams choose their alternatives, their next set of choices is determined. Teams debate their various options before each move, and on each team a team historian records the possible choices and the reasoning behind each move in the simulation as well as the random events generated by the computer. At the conclusion of the simulation, teams compare their scores, based on how well they achieved their original objectives. Then the class discusses what they learned about the results of employing power in different ways and how making different choices really did lead to different results. As the period ends, Sharon observes that if the British had responded differently to the demands of the colonists, we might not have to study United States history in the eleventh grade.

For homework, Crawford poses a series of historical and contemporary situations in which a specific government's decisions produced certain results. He includes the American Revolution, the Bolshevik Revolution of 1917, the Soviet-Baltic conflict, and the conflict in Northern Ireland. Each student compares his or her findings from the simulation to the four situations and suggests how alternative government policies may have resulted in different outcomes. Crawford evaluates the written responses recorded in the team historian's log on the basis of clear and cogent reasoning, establishment of direct linkages between causes and proposed effects, and analysis of the relationship between government philosophies and policy choices.

Sampler of *Curriculum Standards for Social Studies*

VII *Production, Distribution, & Consumption*

Social studies programs should include experiences that provide for the study of *how people organize for the production, distribution, and consumption of goods and services*, so that the learner can:

| **Performance Expectations** | **Related Themes** |

a.   give and explain examples of ways that economic systems structure choices about how goods and services are to be produced and distributed;   **I** **III** **VI**

b.   describe the role that supply and demand, prices, incentives, and profits play in determining what is produced and distributed in a competitive market;   **V** **VI** **IX**

c.   explain the difference between private and public goods and services;   **V** **VI**

d.   describe a range of examples of the various institutions that make up economic systems such as households, business firms, banks, government agencies, labor unions, and corporations;   **V** **IX**

e.   describe the role of specialization and exchange in the economic process;   **V** **VIII** **IX**

f.   explain and illustrate how values and beliefs influence different economic decisions;   **I** **IX**

g.   differentiate among various forms of exchange and money;   **I** **IX**

h.   compare basic economic systems according to who determines what is produced, distributed, and consumed;   **I** **V** **VI** **IX**

i.   use economic concepts to help explain historical and current developments and issues in local, national, or global contexts;   **I** **II** **IX**

j.   use economic reasoning to compare different proposals for dealing with a contemporary social issue such as unemployment, acid rain, or high quality education.   **V** **VI** **VIII** **IX** **X**

FOCUS ON THE CLASSROOM: STANDARDS INTO PRACTICE

Performance Expectations: a, e, f, h, i

Patti Barbes' sixth graders use the newspaper as a primary text for their work in social studies, language arts, science, and health. Recent articles have stressed problems related to the availability of adequate food supplies in parts of Africa, in economically distressed regions of the United States, and in the local community.

Barbes recognizes that her students do not have an understanding of the problems associated with making decisions dealing with distribution of limited food supplies. She divides the class into six working groups and gives each group an apple. Each group must decide who will get the apple. There are initial shouts of "Me! Me! Me!" In one group, the first person to grab the apple refuses to give it up. These initial reactions give way to intense discussions about dividing the apples. A coin toss is proposed, and one group tries to determine who has the greatest need.

After each group shares its solutions and its difficulties in coming to a conclusion, Barbes asks each student to consider how the group's deliberations might have been different if they all were experiencing a very limited and inadequate diet. After students write their reactions in their journals, Barbes leads a discussion of their reactions.

This activity is used as a reference point in discussions of related news stories in the weeks ahead. Some students elect to do volunteer work at a local food distribution center, sharing their experiences and observations with the class.

Science, Technology, & Society

Social studies programs should include experiences that provide for the study of *relationships among science, technology, and society*, so that the learner can:

Performance Expectations

Related Themes

a. examine and describe the influence of culture on scientific and technological choices and advancement, such as in transportation, medicine, and warfare;

b. show through specific examples how science and technology have changed people's perceptions of the social and natural world, such as in their relationship to the land, animal life, family life, and economic needs, wants, and security;

c. describe examples in which values, beliefs, and attitudes have been influenced by new scientific and technological knowledge, such as the invention of the printing press, conceptions of the universe, applications of atomic energy, and genetic discoveries;

d. explain the need for laws and policies to govern scientific and technological applications, such as in the safety and well-being of workers and consumers and the regulation of utilities, radio, and television;

e. seek reasonable and ethical solutions to problems that arise when scientific advancements and social norms or values come into conflict.

FOCUS ON THE CLASSROOM: STANDARDS INTO PRACTICE

Performance Expectations: b, c

Lynn Fuller-Bailie's sixth graders are computer game junkies who are not the least bit intimidated by computers, laserdiscs, or interactive video. They take the world of computer technology for granted. In fact, they can't believe how ancient societies and cultures existed without the modern conveniences they have grown to love and need. Fuller-Bailie wants them to understand that science and technology are not just the province of the late twentieth century.

Fuller-Bailie borrows some art prints of the Seven Wonders of the World from Alice Walters, the art teacher. Walters knows how to make slides from the prints and agrees to work with Fuller-Bailie on this project. Walters makes two sets of slides of each of the Seven Wonders: the Temple of Artemis, the Statue of Zeus, the Pyramids of Egypt, the Lighthouse at Alexandria, the Hanging Gardens of Babylon, the Mausoleum of Halicarnassus, and the Colossus of Rhodes. The students in Fuller-Bailie's class are charged with finding out what technologies permitted the people to build these architectural wonders and how these technologies

---

challenged and changed the environment. Fuller-Bailie wants the students to re-evaluate the Seven Wonders in relation to subsequent structures. She begins collecting photos and pictures of Frank Lloyd Wright buildings, the Golden Gate Bridge, the Sears Tower, the Eiffel Tower, the TransAmerican Pyramid, the Tokyo Cathedral, a geodesic dome, the Great Wall of China, and the Washington Monument. Students are to come up with a revised list of Seven Wonders and justify the replacement of any of the original wonders.

In Walters's art class, the students build replicas of the Seven Wonders and design a structure of their own that is worth being called an Eighth Wonder. They describe the technology necessary to build their wonder and consider the costs and benefits to society. Walters evaluates each student's project on its creativity and aesthetic qualities. Fuller-Bailie evaluates the written part of the assignment using three criteria: analysis of the relationship between technology and building structure, the description of the potential impact of those technologies on the environment, and clarity of writing, including the use of correct grammar and spelling.

Global Connections

Social studies programs should include experiences that provide for the study of *global connections and interdependence*, so that the learner can:

Performance Expectations	Related Themes

a.   describe instances in which language, art, music, belief systems, and other cultural elements can facilitate global understanding or cause misunderstanding;

I **II** **III**

b.   analyze examples of conflict, cooperation, and interdependence among groups, societies, and nations;

V **VI**

c.   describe and analyze the effects of changing technologies on the global community;

VIII

d.   explore the causes, consequences, and possible solutions to persistent, contemporary, and emerging global issues, such as health, security, resource allocation, economic development, and environmental quality;

III **VIII**

e.   describe and explain the relationships and tensions between national sovereignty and global interest in such matters as territory, natural resources, trade, use of technology, and welfare of people;

V **VI** **VIII**

f.   demonstrate understanding of concerns, standards, issues, and conflicts related to universal human rights;

VI **X**

g.   identify and describe the roles of international and multinational organizations.

V **VII**

FOCUS ON THE CLASSROOM: STANDARDS INTO PRACTICE

Performance Expectations: b, d, g

   Margi Rodriquez prepares a list of businesses and organizations in the city, trying to include as many as possible of those who have been involved in education or have supported the school system in the past. She and her seventh grade social studies students construct a brief survey to identify ways in which these businesses or organizations have global connections. Students select one of the businesses or organizations to contact and survey. Rodriguez assists students in developing the confidence necessary to approach the proper individuals to request time from their busy schedules for an interview.

   With the exception of a few predictable rough spots, students are successful in completing their surveys. They then compile their findings and discover both expected and unexpected patterns regarding the global connections that exist in the local business community. They find that some companies have foreign workers, use equipment or parts originating outside the United States, have parent or satellite companies in other countries, or export their products or services to other countries. Each student develops a poster or graphic that illustrates either the information gathered by that student or a compilation of the findings of the class. To accompany the graphic, each student also prepares a brief statement in the form of a news story, which is videotaped and shared with the company each student contacted. Accuracy and quality of presentation, thoroughness of effort to identify ways in which the assigned company has global connections, and analysis of data serve as criteria to evaluate evidence of understanding.

X *Civic Ideals & Practices*

Social studies programs should include experiences that provide for the study of *the ideals, principles, and practices of citizenship in a democratic republic*, so that the learner can:

Performance Expectations   **Related Themes**

a.   examine the origins and continuing influences of key ideals of the   **II** **V** **VI**
democratic republican form of government, such as individual human dignity,
liberty, justice, equality, and the rule of law;

b.   identify and interpret sources and examples of the rights and   **II**
responsibilities of citizens;

c.   locate, access, analyze, organize, and apply information about selected   **I** **II** **V** **IX**
public issues—recognizing and explaining multiple points of view;

d.   practice forms of civic discussion and participation consistent with the   **II** **V** **VI**
ideals of citizens in a democratic republic;

e.   explain and analyze various forms of citizen action that influence public   **I** **V** **VI**
policy decisions;

f.   identify and explain the roles of formal and informal political actors in   **V** **VI**
influencing and shaping public policy and decision-making;

g.   analyze the influence of diverse forms of public opinion on the   **V** **VI**
development of public policy and decision-making;

h.   analyze the effectiveness of selected public policies and citizen behaviors **II** **V** **VI** **IX**
in realizing the stated ideals of a democratic republican form of government;

i.   explain the relationship between policy statements and action plans used   **VI**
to address issues of public concern;

j.   examine strategies designed to strengthen the "common good," which   **II** **V** **VI**
consider a range of options for citizen action.

FOCUS ON THE CLASSROOM: STANDARDS INTO PRACTICE

Performance Expectation: b, c, d, h, i
    As a part of a unit on the powers and duties of the executive branch, Suzanne Kim gives her eighth-grade students a news article about President Clinton's process of appointing an Attorney General. Both of those whom he initially proposed found themselves in an awkward position because they had hired illegal immigrants

(undocumented workers) to serve as babysitters for their children while they worked. Although most of the discussion in the article is about the problems that women face in finding childcare, Kim wants her students to focus on the question "Who is a citizen and what does it take to become one?"

Kim passes out a list with the following on it:

Who is a citizen? How do you know?

1. A baby is born in Mexico while her parents, who are U.S. citizens, are on vacation. What is her citizenship?

2. A Jamaican woman has worked for many years in this country but has never applied for citizenship. This past year she married a U.S. citizen.

3. Refugees flee an oppressive, non-democratic government with which the United States has no diplomatic relations. The president tells the people of that nation that they can seek political asylum here. Are the refugees citizens? If not, are they eligible for citizenship?

4. Refugees flee an oppressive, non-democratic government with which the United States does have diplomatic relations. The president discourages these people from immigrating to the United States, saying that they are merely fleeing for economic purposes. Are these refugees citizens? If not, are they eligible to become citizens?

5. You emigrate to France. You have no intentions of returning to the United States. You no longer file U.S. income tax returns. Of which country are you a citizen?

6. A husband and wife have been undocumented workers in the United States for seven years. They have a baby. Is the baby a U.S. citizen?

Students work in small groups to discuss who is a citizen and what it takes to become a citizen. Kim arranges for a speaker from the Immigration and Naturalization Service to speak to her class the next day. Following this, the class analyzes current U.S. immigration policy in light of America's historical commitment to the ideals of justice and fairness.

Each student then writes an editorial appropriate for a specific newspaper of his or her choice, explaining the pros and cons of U.S. immigration policy and defending a position related to the policy. The editorials are evaluated on: accurate representation of contemporary immigration policy; the student's ability to analyze this policy in the light of the historical ideals and current practices discussed; development of a logical argument; and the student's success in choosing the appropriate tone for the selected newspaper.